Q&A a Day for Kids is a special journ[...]
your child every day for three years. T[...] [...]
not only lets you see the evolution of his or her answers, but
it also becomes a time capsule of your child's life.

Because the questions in this book were written for kids
between the ages of three and ten, some questions might
be a bit advanced for the youngest children. You can always
reword them to make them more appropriate. If you and
your child interpret a question differently, going with his
interpretation will likely be more fun and more interesting.

Depending on the age of your son or daughter, you may be
sitting with your child as he or she dictates. Or she may
take over the book and write in it on her own. Some of
your child's answers may delight you. Some may surprise
you. Some may even concern you. To have a true record,
you may want to hold back from commenting and just see
where your child is and where he goes.

What an adventure it is to witness your child's developing
and deepening thoughts and feelings over three years! In
some ways, a child may change dramatically, and in others,
she may remain essentially the same. **Q&A a Day for Kids**
is a wonderful way for children to get to know themselves
and for you as a parent to witness and record the process.

JANUARY  01

Write your name.

20_ _ _____

_____

_____

_____

20_ _ _____

_____

_____

_____

20_ _ _____

_____

_____

_____

JANUARY  02

What is your favorite
thing to do with friends?

20_ _ _ _____

_____

_____

_____

_____

20_ _ _ _____

_____

_____

_____

_____

20_ _ _ _____

_____

_____

_____

_____

JANUARY 03

What are you excited about?

20__ __ _____

_____

_____

_____

20__ __ _____

_____

_____

_____

20__ __ _____

_____

_____

_____

JANUARY  04

Which animal do you feel like today? Why?

20___ _____

_____

_____

_____

_____

20___ _____

_____

_____

_____

_____

20___ _____

_____

_____

_____

_____

JANUARY  05

Describe a time when you were mad.

20__ __

_____
_____
_____
_____
_____

20__ __

_____
_____
_____
_____
_____

20__ __

_____
_____
_____
_____
_____

JANUARY 06

If you could take a trip anywhere in the world, where would you go?

20___ _____

_____

_____

_____

_____

20___ _____

_____

_____

_____

_____

20___ _____

_____

_____

_____

_____

JANUARY  07

What would you like to
do but can't do yet?

20___ _____

_____

_____

_____

20___ _____

_____

_____

_____

20___ _____

_____

_____

_____

_____

JANUARY  08

Who is your hero? Why?

20__ _____

_____

_____

_____

_____

20__ _____

_____

_____

_____

_____

20__ _____

_____

_____

_____

_____

JANUARY 09

I wish I had more _____.

20___ _____

_____

_____

_____

20___ _____

_____

_____

_____

20___ _____

_____

_____

_____

JANUARY  10

What are you especially good at?

20_ _ _____

_____

_____

_____

_____

20_ _ _____

_____

_____

_____

_____

20_ _ _____

_____

_____

_____

_____

JANUARY  11

Has anyone ever called
you a name? Tell about it.

20___ _____

_____

_____

_____

_____

20___ _____

_____

_____

_____

_____

20___ _____

_____

_____

_____

_____

JANUARY

12 How do you feel when friends play with your things?

20__ _____

_____

_____

_____

20__ _____

_____

_____

_____

20__ _____

_____

_____

_____

JANUARY 13

_____ is a silly thing I did lately.

20__ __ _____

_____

_____

_____

_____

20__ __ _____

_____

_____

_____

_____

20__ __ _____

_____

_____

_____

_____

JANUARY  14

Who helps you when you're sad?

20__ __ _____

_____

_____

_____

20__ __ _____

_____

_____

_____

20__ __ _____

_____

_____

_____

JANUARY  15

If you could buy anything, what would you buy?

20__ __ _____

_____

_____

_____

_____

20__ __ _____

_____

_____

_____

_____

20__ __ _____

_____

_____

_____

_____

JANUARY  16

I felt awful when _____.

20___ _____

_____

_____

_____

_____

20___ _____

_____

_____

_____

_____

20___ _____

_____

_____

_____

_____

JANUARY  17

What did you have the most fun doing today?

20__ __ _____

_____

_____

_____

_____

20__ __ _____

_____

_____

_____

_____

20__ __ _____

_____

_____

_____

_____

JANUARY  18

What sounds do you
hear around you?

20_ _

_____

_____

_____

_____

_____

20_ _

_____

_____

_____

_____

_____

20_ _

_____

_____

_____

_____

_____

JANUARY  19

How do you feel about babysitters?

20___ _____

_____

_____

_____

_____

20___ _____

_____

_____

_____

_____

20___ _____

_____

_____

_____

_____

JANUARY  20

Describe your favorite snack and the place you like to eat it.

20__ _____

_____

_____

_____

20__ _____

_____

_____

_____

20__ _____

_____

_____

_____

JANUARY  21

Do you believe in aliens?
Explain.

20__
_____
_____
_____
_____
_____

20__
_____
_____
_____
_____

20__
_____
_____
_____
_____

JANUARY  22

What makes you feel special?

20_ _ _____

_____

_____

_____

_____

20_ _ _____

_____

_____

_____

_____

20_ _ _____

_____

_____

_____

_____

JANUARY  23

Did anyone bug you today? If so, how?

20___ _____

_____

_____

_____

_____

20___ _____

_____

_____

_____

_____

20___ _____

_____

_____

_____

_____

JANUARY

I make a good friend because _____.

20__ __ _____

_____

_____

_____

_____

20__ __ _____

_____

_____

_____

_____

20__ __ _____

_____

_____

_____

_____

JANUARY  25

How do you feel about sitting at the dinner table?

20____ _____

_____

_____

_____

_____

20____ _____

_____

_____

_____

_____

20____ _____

_____

_____

_____

_____

JANUARY 26

I'm worried about _____.

20__ __ _____

_____

_____

_____

_____

20__ __ _____

_____

_____

_____

_____

20__ __ _____

_____

_____

_____

_____

JANUARY  27

What have you done lately that you're proud of?

20_ _
_____

_____

_____

_____

20_ _
_____

_____

_____

_____

20_ _
_____

_____

_____

_____

JANUARY  28

When you look in the
mirror, what do you see?

20___ _____

_____

_____

_____

_____

20___ _____

_____

_____

_____

_____

20___ _____

_____

_____

_____

_____

JANUARY

What jobs look
interesting to you?

20_ _ _____

_____

_____

_____

_____

20_ _ _____

_____

_____

_____

_____

_____

20_ _ _____

_____

_____

_____

_____

JANUARY  30

Which book character would you like to meet?

20__ _____

_____

_____

_____

_____

20__ _____

_____

_____

_____

_____

20__ _____

_____

_____

_____

_____

JANUARY  31

What was the most boring part of school today?

20__ _____

_____

_____

_____

_____

20__ _____

_____

_____

_____

_____

20__ _____

_____

_____

_____

_____

FEBRUARY  01

What do you hope for?

20___ _____

_____

_____

_____

_____

20___ _____

_____

_____

_____

_____

20___ _____

_____

_____

_____

_____

FEBRUARY  02

Which toys do you like
to take to bed?

20_ _ _____

_____

_____

_____

_____

20_ _ _____

_____

_____

_____

_____

20_ _ _____

_____

_____

_____

_____

FEBRUARY  03

Describe a time you felt bad for someone else.

20___ _____

_____

_____

_____

_____

20___ _____

_____

_____

_____

_____

20___ _____

_____

_____

_____

_____

FEBRUARY  04

What are you thankful for today?

20__ _____

_____

_____

_____

_____

20__ _____

_____

_____

_____

_____

20__ _____

_____

_____

_____

_____

FEBRUARY  05

What is your favorite
thing in nature?

20___ _____

_____

_____

_____

_____

20___ _____

_____

_____

_____

_____

20___ _____

_____

_____

_____

_____

FEBRUARY  06

When was the last time you felt shy or quiet? Why?

20_ _ _

_____

_____

_____

_____

_____

20_ _ _

_____

_____

_____

_____

_____

20_ _ _

_____

_____

_____

_____

_____

FEBRUARY  07

I like it when my
family _____ together.

20__ __ _____

_____

_____

_____

_____

20__ __ _____

_____

_____

_____

_____

20__ __ _____

_____

_____

_____

_____

FEBRUARY

08 What rules at school don't make sense to you?

20__ __ _____

_____

_____

_____

_____

20__ __ _____

_____

_____

_____

_____

20__ __ _____

_____

_____

_____

_____

FEBRUARY  09

What's your favorite lunch?

20___ _____

_____

_____

_____

_____

20___ _____

_____

_____

_____

_____

20___ _____

_____

_____

_____

_____

FEBRUARY  10

I'm glad the book character _____ is not real.

20____ _____

_____

_____

_____

_____

20____ _____

_____

_____

_____

_____

20____ _____

_____

_____

_____

_____

FEBRUARY  11

Have you ever
taught someone else
something? What?

20___ _____

_____

_____

_____

_____

20___ _____

_____

_____

_____

_____

20___ _____

_____

_____

_____

_____

FEBRUARY  12

What would you hate to lose?

20__ __ _____

_____

_____

_____

_____

20__ __ _____

_____

_____

_____

_____

20__ __ _____

_____

_____

_____

_____

FEBRUARY

13 If you buried a treasure chest, what would be in it?

20__ _____

_____

_____

_____

_____

20__ _____

_____

_____

_____

_____

20__ _____

_____

_____

_____

_____

FEBRUARY  14

What do you really like about yourself today?

20__ __

_____

_____

_____

_____

_____

20__ __

_____

_____

_____

_____

_____

20__ __

_____

_____

_____

_____

_____

FEBRUARY  15

What is your favorite
sport? Why?

20__ _____

_____

_____

_____

_____

20__ _____

_____

_____

_____

_____

20__ _____

_____

_____

_____

_____

FEBRUARY  16

I know I can _____ on my own, but no one else thinks so.

20__ __ _____

_____

_____

_____

_____

20__ __ _____

_____

_____

_____

_____

20__ __ _____

_____

_____

_____

_____

FEBRUARY

What did you do this week to keep your body strong and healthy?

20___ _____

_____

_____

_____

_____

20___ _____

_____

_____

_____

_____

20___ _____

_____

_____

_____

_____

FEBRUARY  18

When were you brave?

20__ _____

_____

_____

_____

_____

20__ _____

_____

_____

_____

_____

20__ _____

_____

_____

_____

_____

FEBRUARY

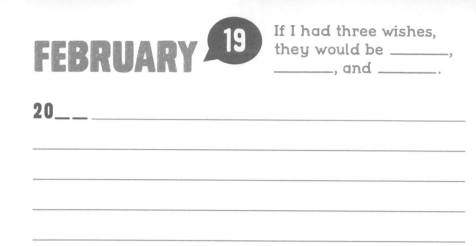

19

If I had three wishes,
they would be _____,
_____, and _____.

20___ _____

_____

_____

_____

_____

20___ _____

_____

_____

_____

_____

20___ _____

_____

_____

_____

_____

FEBRUARY

20 When did you feel like lying, but told the truth?

20__ _____

_____

_____

_____

_____

20__ _____

_____

_____

_____

_____

20__ _____

_____

_____

_____

_____

FEBRUARY

Tell about a time you helped someone.

20_ _ _____

_____

_____

_____

_____

20_ _ _____

_____

_____

_____

_____

20_ _ _____

_____

_____

_____

_____

FEBRUARY

22 Describe what one of your parents does for a job.

20_ _ _____

_____

_____

_____

_____

20_ _ _____

_____

_____

_____

_____

20_ _ _____

_____

_____

_____

_____

FEBRUARY

23 What advice do you have about keeping a friend?

20_ _ _____

_____

_____

_____

_____

20_ _ _____

_____

_____

_____

_____

20_ _ _____

_____

_____

_____

_____

FEBRUARY  24

When do you feel peaceful and calm?

20__ _____

_____

_____

_____

_____

20__ _____

_____

_____

_____

_____

20__ _____

_____

_____

_____

_____

FEBRUARY

What is your favorite TV show?

20___ _____

_____

_____

_____

_____

20___ _____

_____

_____

_____

_____

20___ _____

_____

_____

_____

_____

FEBRUARY  26

Which noises bother you?

20__ __ _____

_____

_____

_____

_____

20__ __ _____

_____

_____

_____

_____

20__ __ _____

_____

_____

_____

_____

FEBRUARY

27 Describe something you would never change about yourself.

20__ __ _____

_____

_____

_____

_____

20__ __ _____

_____

_____

_____

_____

20__ __ _____

_____

_____

_____

_____

FEBRUARY  28

Which one of your senses (seeing, hearing, smelling, touching, or tasting) is your favorite? Why?

20___ _____

_____

_____

_____

_____

20___ _____

_____

_____

_____

_____

20___ _____

_____

_____

_____

_____

FEBRUARY  29

Is this a leap year?
Did anything unusual
happen today?

20__ __ _____

_____

_____

_____

_____

20__ __ _____

_____

_____

_____

_____

20__ __ _____

_____

_____

_____

_____

MARCH  01

What is the best thing about a rainy day?

20__ __ _____

_____

_____

_____

_____

20__ __ _____

_____

_____

_____

_____

20__ __ _____

_____

_____

_____

_____

MARCH  02

What is hard for you to do?

20__ __ _____

_____

_____

_____

_____

20__ __ _____

_____

_____

_____

_____

20__ __ _____

_____

_____

_____

_____

MARCH  03

Who taught you something you really wanted to know? What was it?

20___ _____

_____

_____

_____

_____

20___ _____

_____

_____

_____

_____

20___ _____

_____

_____

_____

_____

MARCH  04

I don't like to wear _____.

20____ _____

_____

_____

_____

_____

20____ _____

_____

_____

_____

_____

20____ _____

_____

_____

_____

_____

MARCH  05

What is the best thing about your life right now?

20___ _____

_____

_____

_____

_____

20___ _____

_____

_____

_____

_____

20___ _____

_____

_____

_____

_____

MARCH  06

Whom do you feel most safe with?

20___ _____

_____

_____

_____

_____

20___ _____

_____

_____

_____

_____

20___ _____

_____

_____

_____

_____

MARCH  07

What does someone else have that you wish you had?

20__ __

20__ __

20__ __

MARCH  08

How do you feel about video games?

20_ _ _____

_____

_____

_____

_____

20_ _ _____

_____

_____

_____

_____

20_ _ _____

_____

_____

_____

_____

MARCH  09

Have you gone anywhere new lately?

20_ _ _____

_____

_____

_____

_____

20_ _ _____

_____

_____

_____

_____

20_ _ _____

_____

_____

_____

_____

MARCH  10

What does the sky look like today?

20__ __ _____

_____

_____

_____

_____

20__ __ _____

_____

_____

_____

_____

20__ __ _____

_____

_____

_____

_____

MARCH  11

What do you wish you had
more time for these days?

20___ _____

_____

_____

_____

_____

20___ _____

_____

_____

_____

_____

20___ _____

_____

_____

_____

_____

MARCH  12

If you ruled the world, what would you change?

20___ _____

_____

_____

_____

_____

20___ _____

_____

_____

_____

_____

20___ _____

_____

_____

_____

_____

MARCH

 **13** Do you like your name? Is there another name you'd rather have?

20__ _____

_____

_____

_____

_____

20__ _____

_____

_____

_____

_____

20__ _____

_____

_____

_____

_____

MARCH  14

Do the clothes you're wearing today feel right for you? Why or why not?

20___ _____

_____

_____

_____

_____

20___ _____

_____

_____

_____

_____

20___ _____

_____

_____

_____

_____

MARCH 15

Name one troublemaker
in your life. Explain.

20__ _____

_____

_____

_____

_____

20__ _____

_____

_____

_____

_____

20__ _____

_____

_____

_____

_____

MARCH  16

What would you do with a giant cardboard box?

20__ __ _____

_____

_____

_____

_____

20__ __ _____

_____

_____

_____

_____

20__ __ _____

_____

_____

_____

_____

MARCH  17

What are you wearing that's green?

20___ ___

_____

_____

_____

_____

20___ ___

_____

_____

_____

_____

20___ ___

_____

_____

_____

_____

MARCH  18

What is your favorite way to get around?

20____ _____

_____

_____

_____

_____

20____ _____

_____

_____

_____

_____

20____ _____

_____

_____

_____

_____

MARCH  19

What is the best part
of your birthday?

20___ _____

_____

_____

_____

_____

20___ _____

_____

_____

_____

_____

20___ _____

_____

_____

_____

_____

MARCH  20

What are the worst jobs you've ever heard of?

20___
_____
_____
_____
_____
_____

20___
_____
_____
_____
_____
_____

20___
_____
_____
_____
_____

MARCH  21

How have you helped your family this week?

20____ _____

_____

_____

_____

_____

20____ _____

_____

_____

_____

_____

20____ _____

_____

_____

_____

_____

MARCH  22

When was the last time you felt embarrassed?

20__ __ _____

_____

_____

_____

_____

20__ __ _____

_____

_____

_____

_____

20__ __ _____

_____

_____

_____

_____

MARCH  23

Whom do you have the most fun with? What do you do together?

20_ _ _____

_____

_____

_____

20_ _ _____

_____

_____

_____

20_ _ _____

_____

_____

_____

MARCH 24

Do you ever get in trouble?
Describe one time.

20___ _____

_____

_____

_____

_____

20___ _____

_____

_____

_____

_____

20___ _____

_____

_____

_____

_____

MARCH  25

Where is your favorite place in nature?

20_ _ _____

_____

_____

_____

_____

20_ _ _____

_____

_____

_____

_____

20_ _ _____

_____

_____

_____

_____

MARCH 26

I complain about _____ a lot.

20_____ _____

20_____ _____

20_____ _____

MARCH  27

What musical instrument do you play or would you like to play?

20___ _____

_____

_____

_____

20___ _____

_____

_____

_____

20___ _____

_____

_____

_____

MARCH

Who is the oldest person you know?

20__ _____

_____

_____

_____

20__ _____

_____

_____

_____

20__ _____

_____

_____

_____

MARCH  29

Have you felt lonely lately? Why?

20___ _____

_____

_____

_____

_____

20___ _____

_____

_____

_____

_____

20___ _____

_____

_____

_____

_____

MARCH  30

What do you see out your window?

20_ _ _____

_____

_____

_____

_____

20_ _ _____

_____

_____

_____

_____

20_ _ _____

_____

_____

_____

_____

MARCH  31

What do you try to forget about but can't?

20_ _ _____

_____

_____

_____

_____

20_ _ _____

_____

_____

_____

_____

20_ _ _____

_____

_____

_____

_____

APRIL  01

Did you play a trick on anyone today? What was it?

20___ _____

_____

_____

_____

_____

20___ _____

_____

_____

_____

_____

20___ _____

_____

_____

_____

_____

APRIL  02

If you could have any superpower, what would it be? Why?

20___ _____

_____

_____

_____

_____

20___ _____

_____

_____

_____

_____

20___ _____

_____

_____

_____

_____

APRIL  03

What is the worst part of having (or not having) a sister or brother?

20_ _ _____

_____

_____

_____

20_ _ _____

_____

_____

_____

20_ _ _____

_____

_____

_____

APRIL 04

What are your favorite clothes to wear?

20__ __ _____

_____

_____

_____

_____

20__ __ _____

_____

_____

_____

_____

20__ __ _____

_____

_____

_____

_____

APRIL

If you could go into the past, where would you go? Why?

20___ _____

_____

_____

_____

_____

20___ _____

_____

_____

_____

_____

20___ _____

_____

_____

_____

_____

APRIL 06

What would you like to tell your mother or another close family member?

20_____

_____

_____

_____

20_____

_____

_____

_____

20_____

_____

_____

_____

_____

APRIL  07

Who understands you the best?

20__ __ _____

_____

_____

_____

_____

20__ __ _____

_____

_____

_____

_____

20__ __ _____

_____

_____

_____

_____

APRIL 08

Are you sad about anything today? What is it?

20___ _____

_____

_____

_____

_____

20___ _____

_____

_____

_____

_____

20___ _____

_____

_____

_____

_____

APRIL 09

If _____, things would be a lot better.

20___ _____

_____

_____

_____

_____

20___ _____

_____

_____

_____

_____

20___ _____

_____

_____

_____

_____

APRIL 10

What have you done lately
to help the planet?

20___ _____

_____

_____

_____

_____

20___ _____

_____

_____

_____

_____

20___ _____

_____

_____

_____

_____

APRIL 11

How much do you think these things cost: a gallon of milk, a car, your sneakers?

20___ _____

_____

_____

_____

_____

20___ _____

_____

_____

_____

_____

20___ _____

_____

_____

_____

_____

APRIL 12

When did you feel left out?

20___ _____

_____

_____

_____

_____

20___ _____

_____

_____

_____

_____

20___ _____

_____

_____

_____

_____

APRIL  13

What is your favorite season? Why?

20__ __ _____

_____

_____

_____

_____

20__ __ _____

_____

_____

_____

_____

20__ __ _____

_____

_____

_____

_____

APRIL 14

I especially love _____ lately.

20__ _____

_____

_____

_____

_____

20__ _____

_____

_____

_____

_____

20__ _____

_____

_____

_____

_____

APRIL  15

Whom do you look up to?
Why?

20_ _ _____

_____

_____

_____

_____

20_ _ _____

_____

_____

_____

_____

20_ _ _____

_____

_____

_____

_____

APRIL  16

Is there something you'd like to do with someone in your family? What is it?

20_ _ _____

_____

_____

_____

_____

20_ _ _____

_____

_____

_____

_____

20_ _ _____

_____

_____

_____

_____

APRIL  17

If you were a dog, what kind would you be?

20__ _____

_____

_____

_____

_____

20__ _____

_____

_____

_____

_____

20__ _____

_____

_____

_____

_____

APRIL 18

I hate it when _____.

20__ _____

_____

_____

_____

_____

20__ _____

_____

_____

_____

_____

20__ _____

_____

_____

_____

_____

APRIL  19

What music makes you happy? Why?

20____ _____

_____

_____

_____

20____ _____

_____

_____

_____

20____ _____

_____

_____

_____

APRIL 20

Did you ever tell a lie? What did you say?

20__ _____

_____

_____

_____

20__ _____

_____

_____

_____

20__ _____

_____

_____

_____

APRIL

Whose mind would you like to be able to read? Why?

20_ _ _____

_____

_____

_____

_____

20_ _ _____

_____

_____

_____

_____

20_ _ _____

_____

_____

_____

_____

APRIL 22

How do you usually get to school?

20_ _ _____

_____

_____

_____

_____

20_ _ _____

_____

_____

_____

_____

20_ _ _____

_____

_____

_____

_____

APRIL  23

How would you describe the place where you live?

20___ _____

_____

_____

_____

_____

20___ _____

_____

_____

_____

_____

20___ _____

_____

_____

_____

_____

APRIL 24

Who helps you when you're afraid?

20___ _____

_____

_____

_____

_____

20___ _____

_____

_____

_____

_____

20___ _____

_____

_____

_____

_____

APRIL 25

When did you feel confident in yourself?

20___ _____
_____
_____
_____
_____

20___ _____
_____
_____
_____
_____

20___ _____
_____
_____
_____
_____

APRIL 26

Whom would you like to be friends with? Why?

20____ _____

_____

_____

_____

_____

20____ _____

_____

_____

_____

_____

20____ _____

_____

_____

_____

_____

APRIL 27

What are you doing after school today?

20_ _ _____

_____

_____

_____

_____

20_ _ _____

_____

_____

_____

_____

20_ _ _____

_____

_____

_____

_____

APRIL  28

What is your favorite color?
What does it remind you of?

20__ _____

_____

_____

_____

_____

20__ _____

_____

_____

_____

_____

20__ _____

_____

_____

_____

_____

APRIL 29

Who lives in your home with you?

20___ _____

_____

_____

_____

_____

20___ _____

_____

_____

_____

_____

20___ _____

_____

_____

_____

_____

APRIL **30**

What is your nickname?
Who uses it?

20___ _____

_____

_____

_____

_____

20___ _____

_____

_____

_____

_____

20___ _____

_____

_____

_____

_____

MAY  01

If you could have any animal for a pet, what would it be?

20___ _____

_____

_____

_____

_____

20___ _____

_____

_____

_____

_____

20___ _____

_____

_____

_____

_____

MAY 02

How did you calm down the last time you were angry?

20___ _____

_____

_____

_____

_____

20___ _____

_____

_____

_____

_____

20___ _____

_____

_____

_____

_____

MAY 03

What do you like to do at recess (or at the park) these days?

20_ _ _____

_____

_____

_____

_____

20_ _ _____

_____

_____

_____

_____

20_ _ _____

_____

_____

_____

_____

MAY 04

Which age would you like to be? Why?

20_ _ _____

_____

_____

_____

_____

20_ _ _____

_____

_____

_____

_____

20_ _ _____

_____

_____

_____

_____

MAY 05

What is your favorite time of day at home?

20___ _____

_____

_____

_____

_____

20___ _____

_____

_____

_____

_____

20___ _____

_____

_____

_____

_____

MAY 06

What do you want right now, but are afraid to ask for?

20___ _____

_____

_____

_____

_____

20___ _____

_____

_____

_____

_____

20___ _____

_____

_____

_____

_____

MAY  07

Are your friends nice to you?
Give an example.

20_ _ _____

_____

_____

_____

_____

20_ _ _____

_____

_____

_____

_____

20_ _ _____

_____

_____

_____

_____

MAY 08

I get frustrated when _____.

20__ _____

20__ _____

20__ _____

MAY 09

Describe an imaginary creature you wish you could meet.

20__ __ _____

_____

_____

_____

_____

20__ __ _____

_____

_____

_____

_____

20__ __ _____

_____

_____

_____

_____

MAY 10

What color of the rainbow do you feel like today? Why?

20___ _____

_____

_____

_____

20___ _____

_____

_____

_____

20___ _____

_____

_____

_____

MAY 11

What would be a good
Mother's Day gift?

20_ _ _____

_____

_____

_____

_____

20_ _ _____

_____

_____

_____

_____

20_ _ _____

_____

_____

_____

_____

MAY 12

How do you feel about sitting still in school?

20__ _____

_____

_____

_____

_____

20__ _____

_____

_____

_____

_____

20__ _____

_____

_____

_____

_____

MAY  13

What person in the world would you like to meet?

20__ __ _____

_____

_____

_____

_____

20__ __ _____

_____

_____

_____

_____

20__ __ _____

_____

_____

_____

_____

MAY **14**

What did you have for lunch today?
Did you like it?

20_____ _____

_____

_____

_____

20_____ _____

_____

_____

_____

20_____ _____

_____

_____

_____

MAY 15

What seems dangerous to you?
Why?

20___ _____

_____

_____

_____

_____

20___ _____

_____

_____

_____

_____

20___ _____

_____

_____

_____

_____

MAY 16

How do you feel when you look at the stars at night?

20___ _____

_____

_____

_____

_____

20___ _____

_____

_____

_____

_____

20___ _____

_____

_____

_____

_____

MAY 17

Do you have enough free time?
Why or why not?

20__ _____

_____

_____

_____

20__ _____

_____

_____

_____

20__ _____

_____

_____

_____

MAY 18

_____ is mean. Explain.

20___ _____

_____

_____

_____

_____

20___ _____

_____

_____

_____

_____

20___ _____

_____

_____

_____

_____

MAY 19

What are your favorite toys? Why?

20_ _ _____

_____

_____

_____

_____

20_ _ _____

_____

_____

_____

_____

20_ _ _____

_____

_____

_____

_____

MAY 20

What is the wildest thing you've ever done?

20___ _____

_____

_____

_____

_____

20___ _____

_____

_____

_____

_____

20___ _____

_____

_____

_____

_____

MAY 21

If you could fly right now, where would you go?

20___ _____

_____

_____

_____

_____

20___ _____

_____

_____

_____

_____

20___ _____

_____

_____

_____

_____

MAY 22

What is your dream job?

20___ _____

_____

_____

_____

_____

20___ _____

_____

_____

_____

_____

20___ _____

_____

_____

_____

_____

MAY  23

How do you like to spend your time on the weekend?

20_ _ _____

_____

_____

_____

_____

20_ _ _____

_____

_____

_____

_____

20_ _ _____

_____

_____

_____

_____

MAY 24

Who drives you crazy? Why?

20___ _____

_____

_____

_____

_____

20___ _____

_____

_____

_____

_____

20___ _____

_____

_____

_____

_____

MAY **25**

Which electronics (cell phone, video games, computer, TV, etc.) do you use the most?

20___ _____

_____

_____

_____

_____

20___ _____

_____

_____

_____

_____

20___ _____

_____

_____

_____

_____

MAY 26

Are you loud, quiet, or in between?

20___

_____

20___

_____

20___

_____

MAY 27

I wish I could _____ all day.

20___ _____

_____

_____

_____

_____

20___ _____

_____

_____

_____

_____

20___ _____

_____

_____

_____

_____

MAY 28

Write three words to describe your family.

20__ _____

_____

_____

_____

_____

20__ _____

_____

_____

_____

_____

20__ _____

_____

_____

_____

_____

MAY 29

I wouldn't want my friends to know that _____.

20__ _____

_____

_____

_____

20__ _____

_____

_____

_____

20__ _____

_____

_____

_____

MAY 30

What is the best movie you've seen lately?

20___ _____

_____

_____

_____

_____

20___ _____

_____

_____

_____

_____

20___ _____

_____

_____

_____

_____

MAY 31

What chores are you supposed to do? How do you feel about them?

20___ _____

_____

_____

_____

_____

20___ _____

_____

_____

_____

_____

20___ _____

_____

_____

_____

_____

JUNE 01

Describe a dream you can remember.

20__ _____

_____

_____

_____

_____

20__ _____

_____

_____

_____

_____

20__ _____

_____

_____

_____

_____

JUNE  02

When was the last time you cried?
What made you sad?

20___ _____

_____

_____

_____

_____

20___ _____

_____

_____

_____

_____

20___ _____

_____

_____

_____

_____

JUNE 03

Which do you like more, being inside or outside? Why?

20__ _____

_____

_____

_____

_____

20__ _____

_____

_____

_____

_____

20__ _____

_____

_____

_____

_____

JUNE  04

What have you tried to say, but no one listens?

20__ __ _____

_____

_____

_____

_____

20__ __ _____

_____

_____

_____

_____

20__ __ _____

_____

_____

_____

_____

JUNE 05

Would you like to be a writer, artist, dancer, musician, or actor? How strongly do you feel about it?

20_ _ _____

_____

_____

_____

_____

20_ _ _____

_____

_____

_____

_____

20_ _ _____

_____

_____

_____

_____

JUNE  06

What smells do you really like?

20____ _____

_____

_____

_____

_____

20____ _____

_____

_____

_____

_____

20____ _____

_____

_____

_____

_____

JUNE  07

What are three words to describe your neighborhood?

20__ __ _____

_____

_____

_____

_____

20__ __ _____

_____

_____

_____

_____

20__ __ _____

_____

_____

_____

_____

JUNE 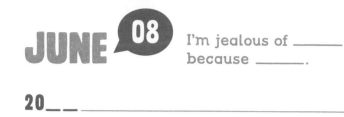 08

I'm jealous of _____ because _____.

20___ _____

_____

_____

_____

_____

20___ _____

_____

_____

_____

_____

20___ _____

_____

_____

_____

_____

JUNE 09

Are you more like sunshine, rain, or thunder? Why?

20____ _____

_____

_____

_____

_____

20____ _____

_____

_____

_____

_____

20____ _____

_____

_____

_____

_____

JUNE 10

Who is the youngest person you know?

20_ _ _____

_____

_____

_____

_____

20_ _ _____

_____

_____

_____

_____

20_ _ _____

_____

_____

_____

_____

JUNE 11

If they made school go all year round, I would _____.

20__ _____

_____

_____

_____

_____

20__ _____

_____

_____

_____

_____

20__ _____

_____

_____

_____

_____

 **JUNE 12**

If you could go back in time and change something, what would it be?

20__ __ _____

_____

_____

_____

20__ __ _____

_____

_____

_____

20__ __ _____

_____

_____

_____

JUNE 13

Do you have any plans with a
friend? What are they?

20__ _____

_____

_____

_____

_____

20__ _____

_____

_____

_____

_____

20__ _____

_____

_____

_____

_____

JUNE 14

I want a new _____ ASAP.

20_ _ _____

_____

_____

_____

_____

20_ _ _____

_____

_____

_____

_____

20_ _ _____

_____

_____

_____

_____

JUNE 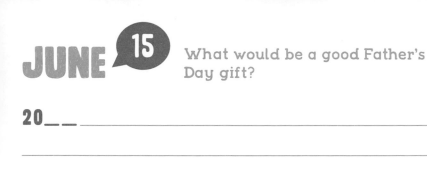 15

What would be a good Father's Day gift?

20__ _____

_____

_____

_____

_____

20__ _____

_____

_____

_____

_____

20__ _____

_____

_____

_____

_____

JUNE 16

Today was fun because _____.

20__ _____

_____

_____

_____

_____

20__ _____

_____

_____

_____

_____

20__ _____

_____

_____

_____

_____

JUNE 17

What do you like best about your face?

20___ _____

_____

_____

_____

20___ _____

_____

_____

_____

20___ _____

_____

_____

_____

JUNE 18

What isn't fair?

20__ _____

_____

_____

_____

_____

20__ _____

_____

_____

_____

_____

20__ _____

_____

_____

_____

_____

JUNE  19

What is a small thing that makes you happy?

20_ _ _ _____

_____

_____

_____

20_ _ _ _____

_____

_____

_____

20_ _ _ _____

_____

_____

_____

JUNE 20

_____ confuses me.

20___ _____

_____

_____

_____

_____

20___ _____

_____

_____

_____

_____

20___ _____

_____

_____

_____

_____

JUNE 21

Is there someone who won't play with you? What's going on?

20_ _ _____

_____

_____

_____

_____

20_ _ _____

_____

_____

_____

_____

20_ _ _____

_____

_____

_____

_____

JUNE  22

Which language would you like to learn? Why?

20___ _____

_____

_____

_____

_____

20___ _____

_____

_____

_____

_____

20___ _____

_____

_____

_____

_____

JUNE 23

What was the last thing you built or made?

20___

20___

20___

JUNE 24

I wish my family was _____.

20__ _____

_____

_____

_____

_____

20__ _____

_____

_____

_____

_____

20__ _____

_____

_____

_____

_____

JUNE 25

Have you ever bullied someone?
What happened?

20__ _____

_____

_____

_____

_____

20__ _____

_____

_____

_____

_____

20__ _____

_____

_____

_____

_____

JUNE  26

Do you like morning or night better? Why?

20___ _____

_____

_____

_____

_____

20___ _____

_____

_____

_____

_____

20___ _____

_____

_____

_____

_____

JUNE 27

What annoys you? Why?

20___ _____

_____

_____

_____

_____

20___ _____

_____

_____

_____

_____

20___ _____

_____

_____

_____

_____

JUNE 28

Is winning important to you?
Why or why not?

20___ _____

_____

_____

_____

_____

20___ _____

_____

_____

_____

_____

20___ _____

_____

_____

_____

_____

JUNE 29

What is the best gift you have ever gotten?

20___ _____

_____

_____

_____

_____

20___ _____

_____

_____

_____

_____

20___ _____

_____

_____

_____

_____

JUNE  30

What makes you feel like crying?

20___ _____

_____

_____

_____

_____

20___ _____

_____

_____

_____

_____

20___ _____

_____

_____

_____

_____

JULY 01

Which relative do you like to talk to? Why?

20_____

_____

_____

_____

_____

20_____

_____

_____

_____

_____

20_____

_____

_____

_____

_____

JULY 02

I feel great when I wear _____.

20_ _ _____

20_ _ _____

20_ _ _____

JULY 03

Is there anything you will NOT eat?

20___ _____

_____

_____

_____

_____

20___ _____

_____

_____

_____

_____

20___ _____

_____

_____

_____

_____

JULY 04

Whom did you play with last?

20_ _ _____

_____

_____

_____

_____

20_ _ _____

_____

_____

_____

_____

20_ _ _____

_____

_____

_____

_____

JULY  05

If you had a day to do whatever you wanted, what would you do?

20__ __ _____

_____

_____

_____

_____

20__ __ _____

_____

_____

_____

_____

20__ __ _____

_____

_____

_____

_____

JULY **06**

Are you afraid of the dark?
Why or why not?

20_ _ _____

_____

_____

_____

_____

20_ _ _____

_____

_____

_____

_____

20_ _ _____

_____

_____

_____

_____

JULY 07

_____ is nice to me. Explain why.

20___

_____

_____

_____

_____

_____

20___

_____

_____

_____

_____

_____

20___

_____

_____

_____

_____

_____

JULY  08

Which three words do you
like the sound of?

20___ _____

_____

_____

_____

_____

20___ _____

_____

_____

_____

_____

20___ _____

_____

_____

_____

_____

JULY 09

Is there something you're sorry you said? What is it?

20_____

_____

_____

_____

_____

20_____

_____

_____

_____

_____

20_____

_____

_____

_____

_____

JULY 10

What's the best thing about today?

20__ _____

_____

_____

_____

_____

20__ _____

_____

_____

_____

_____

20__ _____

_____

_____

_____

_____

JULY

11

When was the last time you wanted to say, "I quit"? Did you?

20___ _____

_____

_____

_____

_____

20___ _____

_____

_____

_____

_____

20___ _____

_____

_____

_____

_____

JULY  12

What snack do other people have that you wish you had?

20___ _____

_____

_____

_____

_____

20___ _____

_____

_____

_____

_____

20___ _____

_____

_____

_____

_____

JULY  13

Do you like surprises or not?
Explain.

20__ __ _____

_____

_____

_____

_____

20__ __ _____

_____

_____

_____

_____

20__ __ _____

_____

_____

_____

_____

If you could help children in another part of the world, what would you do?

20___ _____

_____

_____

_____

_____

20___ _____

_____

_____

_____

_____

20___ _____

_____

_____

_____

_____

JULY 15

What was the last book you liked?

20_ _ _____

20_ _ _____

20_ _ _____

JULY 16

Do you have any new friends?
Who are they?

20**17** Carson, ~~Hazel~~ Hazel, adein.

20___

20___

JULY 17

What is your favorite junk food?

20[1][7] WOPPERS to BC eysagt,

20___

20___

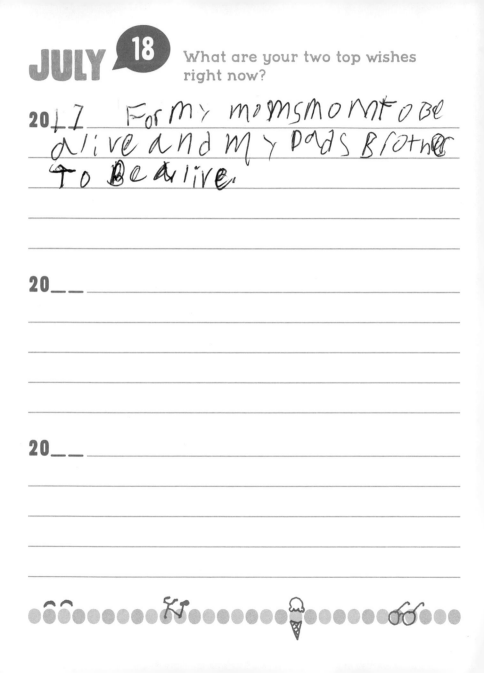

JULY 18

What are your two top wishes right now?

20 17 For my momsmomtobe alive and my Dads Brother to be alive.

20___

20___

JULY 19

Do you like to feel safe,
or do you like adventure?

20_1_ safefursher!!!!!

20___

20___

JULY 20

_Im_ is so funny!

20 17 Im

20___

20___

JULY 21

How would you like to decorate your room?

20 17 Paint Pupal and ~~orange~~
orange

20__ _____

20__ _____

JULY 22

What do you think about when you wake up?

20_17_ What I'm going to do today?

20____

20____

JULY 23

What do you own that is very valuable to you?

20_17_ MY BrOthers.

20___

20___

JULY 24

Have you had a nightmare lately?
Describe it.

20_17_ no.

20___

20___

JULY 25

If only I had _____, then I'd be a lot happier.

20 LY _____ Sister.

20___ _____

20___ _____

JULY 26

Describe your pet or a pet you'd like to have.

20_1_7   a pet Snake.

20___

20___

JULY 27

What have you bought with
your own money lately?

20_17_   nothing

20___

20___

JULY  28

Does anyone fight in your house?
What is that like?

20<u>17</u> no

20___

20___

How do you feel when you see a spider?

20_11_ I time to D o my Dutey.

20___

20___

JULY 30

Who is the last adult you talked to besides a parent?

20_15_ MY unkie.

20____

20____

JULY 31

Write three words to describe your best friend.

20 21 COOL awesome
        smart. LOL this is adout
two friends

20__

20__

AUGUST 01

I wish I could stay up until _____.

20 17 _____ 10:45 _____

20___ _____

20___ _____

AUGUST 02

Would you rather be camping or watching a movie?

20 17   Both.

20__ _____

20__ _____

AUGUST

How do you feel when you're
playing an instrument or
painting a picture?

20_17_ *CIUR IRS...?????

20___

20___

AUGUST 04

Do you feel safer when you're alone or with other people? Explain.

20_1_7_ Other PeoPle.

20___

20___

AUGUST 05

What song fits you? Why?

20_17_ all songs
I'm Ryder.

20___

20___

AUGUST 06

What treasures have you
found lately?

20___ nouthning.

20___

20___

AUGUST  07

If you could be best in the world at something, what would it be?

20**17** _acting._

20__ _____

20__ _____

AUGUST  08

Is someone mad at you?
Who? Why?

20▮▮　　No

20___

20___

AUGUST 09

What do you collect?

20 17 ~~#~~ everything

20___

20___

AUGUST  10

When was the last time you went to a friend's house?

20_1_7_   4 mouths ago.

20___

20___

AUGUST 11

What would you like to learn to do?

20**17** _to Sing._

20____ _____

20____ _____

AUGUST 12

How do you feel about swearing? Explain.

20 11   I Bount like it.

20___

20___

AUGUST 13

What wild thing would you like to do but don't?

20_17_ Naked and ~~afraid~~ afraid.

20___

20___

AUGUST  14

What games do you like to play?

20_17_   tag

20___

20___

AUGUST 15

How do you feel about waking up in the morning?

20_1_7_ ___ O-K ___

20___ ___

20___ ___

AUGUST 16

Describe a time you were sick.

20_1_7_ _____ throwup.

20___ _____

20___ _____

AUGUST 17

Would you rather travel back in time or go to outer space? Why?

20_17_ Back in time
tofixs my Mustaks.

20___

20___

AUGUST 18

How do you feel about sleepovers?

20_17_ Fwmnn!!!

20___

20___

AUGUST

19 Would you rather get something done or hang out and relax?

20_1_7_ get it Done.

20___

20___

20_17_ MY BWANKY.

20___

20___

AUGUST 21

What makes you laugh?

20_1_7_ me aBuyu.

20____

20____

When did you try something
new? What was it?

20_I_ Dout remember

20___

20___

AUGUST 23

How do you feel about brothers and sisters?

20_17_ love it!!!!

20___

20___

AUGUST **24** Did you hurt yourself lately? What happened?

2012 a lump in my leg

20__

20__

AUGUST 25

Do you like someone a lot?
Who is it?

20_17_ Meridith

20___

20___

AUGUST 26

No one knows I _am_.

20_17_ no one knows i am
super smart ☆☆☆

AUGUST 27

What bugs do you like?
What bugs do you dislike?

20 12 i like laDYBugs
i halt laby Bugs.
fla e

20__ __

20__ __

AUGUST 28

I didn't expect _____.

20_17_ i didn't expect
Life??

20___

20___

AUGUST  29

Do you like to play with one person or lots of people?

20__ yesi Do

20__

20__

●●●●●●●●●●●●●●●●●●●●●●●●●●●●●●●●●●●●●

AUGUST 30

What rules at home
seem silly to you?

20_1_7_ every rule. ♡♡♡

AUGUST **31**

What song do you like
to sing? Why?

20**17** What if's BY lune
Brown im good at
singing it

20___

20___

SEPTEMBER

01

Is there something you can't stop thinking about? What is it?

20_1_7_ what LIFE is

20___

20___

SEPTEMBER 02

Do you like to cook?
What is your favorite
thing to make?

20_17_ yes i do, cake
or diserts

20___

20___

SEPTEMBER **03**

Whom do you like to hug? Why?

2017   my Lovely mommy

20__ __

20__ __

SEPTEMBER

04

Is it easy for you to tell people, "No, I don't want to do that"? Or is it hard?

20_17_   yes it is hard

20___

20___

SEPTEMBER 05

The worst part about my bedroom is _my Bedroom_

20_12_ my Bedroom

20___

20___

SEPTEMBER

06 Are you a leader or a follower?

20_11_   Follower

20___

20___

SEPTEMBER 07

If people could see inside you, what would they see?

20_17_ my memories that i cant rememmBer

20___

20___

SEPTEMBER

20_17_ ~~the~~ cars
Boring

20___

20___

SEPTEMBER

09 When do you feel really good about yourself?

20_1_7_ Being nice

20_____

20_____

SEPTEMBER **10**

What do you do to take care of yourself when you're afraid?

20_1_2_   Hide

20___

20___

SEPTEMBER 11

11 Would you rather draw or ride a bike?

20_17_ Draw Duyu

20___

20___

SEPTEMBER  12

Whom would you love to have sitting in your room talking to you?

20_17_ *me*

20___

20___

●●●●●●●●●●●●●●●●●●●●●●●●●●●●●●●●●●●

SEPTEMBER 13

What makes you
nervous? Why?

20_1_7_ telling a girl
i like her. excouse

SEPTEMBER 14

What do you do if someone won't share?

20_17_ leave

20___

20___

SEPTEMBER 15

What is your favorite drink? Why?

20[7 Dr.P or orange Soda. ther so good.

20__

20__

SEPTEMBER 16

Who seems brave to you? Why?

20_1_7_ ~~nope~~

20___

20___

SEPTEMBER 17

How do you feel about homework?

20 17   iT SUCKS
SO BadlY

20___

20___

SEPTEMBER

18

———— doesn't
understand me.
Explain.

20 1 7 _mom_

20 _ _

20 _ _

SEPTEMBER 19

Who is the silliest person you know? Why?

2012 ~~Amwife~~ ~~Amwife~~
m~~y~~ Freinds

20__

20__

SEPTEMBER 20

Do you like to get dirty or not? How come?

20_1_7_ yes, DY

20_ _ _

20_ _ _

SEPTEMBER **21**

Do you feel like a lucky person? Why or why not?

20_1_Z_ no mo nor
your B's

20___

20___

SEPTEMBER 22

What kinds of animals do you like?

20_17_ All animals

20____

20____

SEPTEMBER 23

The best thing about being a grown-up is _____.

20_17_ I know DON4

20___

20___

SEPTEMBER 24

What kinds of books do you like to read?

20_1_7 COMICS

20___

20___

SEPTEMBER  25

Has someone ever asked you to do something you didn't want to do? Explain.

20__ _____

_____

_____

_____

_____

20__ _____

_____

_____

_____

_____

20__ _____

_____

_____

_____

_____

SEPTEMBER  26

What did you have
for breakfast today?

20___ _____

_____

_____

_____

_____

20___ _____

_____

_____

_____

_____

20___ _____

_____

_____

_____

_____

SEPTEMBER  27

I used to dislike
_____, but now
I think I like it.

20_ _ _____

_____

_____

_____

20_ _ _____

_____

_____

_____

20_ _ _____

_____

_____

_____

SEPTEMBER  28

What chores do you always put off?

20___ _____

_____

_____

_____

_____

20___ _____

_____

_____

_____

_____

20___ _____

_____

_____

_____

_____

SEPTEMBER  29

Who loves you a lot?

20_ _ _____

_____

_____

_____

_____

20_ _ _____

_____

_____

_____

_____

20_ _ _____

_____

_____

_____

_____

SEPTEMBER

Which do you like better—math or reading?

20_ _ _____

_____

_____

_____

20_ _ _____

_____

_____

_____

20_ _ _____

_____

_____

_____

_____

OCTOBER 01

Whom are you worried about? Why?

20___ _____

_____

_____

_____

_____

20___ _____

_____

_____

_____

_____

20___ _____

_____

_____

_____

_____

OCTOBER

02 What would your perfect day be like?

20__ _____

_____

_____

_____

20__ _____

_____

_____

_____

20__ _____

_____

_____

_____

OCTOBER  03

I wish my teachers would
_____.

20_ _ _____
_____
_____
_____
_____

20_ _ _____
_____
_____
_____
_____

20_ _ _____
_____
_____
_____
_____

OCTOBER

04

If you could start a company that made something, what would it make?

20___ _____

_____

_____

_____

20___ _____

_____

_____

_____

20___ _____

_____

_____

_____

OCTOBER 05

Do you get allowance?
How do you feel about it?

20___ _____

_____

_____

_____

_____

20___ _____

_____

_____

_____

_____

20___ _____

_____

_____

_____

_____

OCTOBER 06

Who is your best friend?

20__ __ _____

_____

_____

_____

_____

20__ __ _____

_____

_____

_____

_____

20__ __ _____

_____

_____

_____

_____

OCTOBER  07

Do you have a favorite picture, poster, or map hanging in your room? Why do you like it?

20__ __ _____

_____

_____

_____

_____

20__ __ _____

_____

_____

_____

_____

20__ __ _____

_____

_____

_____

_____

OCTOBER  08

_____ really tires me out.

20__ _____

_____

_____

_____

_____

20__ _____

_____

_____

_____

_____

20__ _____

_____

_____

_____

_____

OCTOBER  09

What do you dream about doing?

20__ _____

_____

_____

_____

_____

20__ _____

_____

_____

_____

_____

20__ _____

_____

_____

_____

_____

OCTOBER  10

Do you ever think about having a girlfriend/ boyfriend? Whom would it be?

20____ _____

_____

_____

_____

_____

20____ _____

_____

_____

_____

_____

20____ _____

_____

_____

_____

_____

OCTOBER 11

What is your favorite dinner?

20__ _____

_____

_____

_____

_____

20__ _____

_____

_____

_____

_____

20__ _____

_____

_____

_____

_____

OCTOBER  12

What did someone tell you that wasn't true?

20__ _____

_____

_____

_____

_____

20__ _____

_____

_____

_____

_____

20__ _____

_____

_____

_____

_____

OCTOBER  13

If I had a magic eraser,
I would erase _____.

20___

_____

_____

_____

_____

20___

_____

_____

_____

_____

20___

_____

_____

_____

_____

OCTOBER  14

Are you more like a monkey, a tiger, a fox, or a rabbit?

20__ __ _____

_____

_____

_____

_____

20__ __ _____

_____

_____

_____

_____

20__ __ _____

_____

_____

_____

_____

OCTOBER 15

I hope no one catches me
_____.

20__ _____
_____
_____
_____
_____

20__ _____
_____
_____
_____
_____

20__ _____
_____
_____
_____
_____

OCTOBER  16

Do you believe in ghosts?
Explain.

20___ _____

_____

_____

_____

_____

20___ _____

_____

_____

_____

_____

20___ _____

_____

_____

_____

_____

OCTOBER  17

Pick a parent. What is the most important thing to that parent?

20_ _ _____

_____

_____

_____

_____

20_ _ _____

_____

_____

_____

_____

20_ _ _____

_____

_____

_____

_____

OCTOBER  18

What is the best present someone could give you right now?

20__ _____

_____

_____

_____

_____

20__ _____

_____

_____

_____

_____

20__ _____

_____

_____

_____

_____

OCTOBER  19

Are you mad at someone?
Whom? Why?

20_ _ _____

_____

_____

_____

_____

20_ _ _____

_____

_____

_____

_____

20_ _ _____

_____

_____

_____

_____

OCTOBER  20

Have you tried anything new lately? What?

20_ _ _____

_____

_____

_____

_____

20_ _ _____

_____

_____

_____

_____

20_ _ _____

_____

_____

_____

_____

OCTOBER 21

Do you have any enemies? Who?

20__ _____

_____

_____

_____

_____

20__ _____

_____

_____

_____

_____

20__ _____

_____

_____

_____

_____

OCTOBER  22

What was the last fruit or veggie you ate?

20_ _ _____

_____

_____

_____

_____

20_ _ _____

_____

_____

_____

_____

20_ _ _____

_____

_____

_____

_____

OCTOBER  23

What would you like to get rid of or throw away?

20__ _____

_____

_____

_____

_____

20__ _____

_____

_____

_____

_____

20__ _____

_____

_____

_____

_____

OCTOBER  24

What was the last movie you saw?

20__ __ _____

_____

_____

_____

_____

20__ __ _____

_____

_____

_____

_____

20__ __ _____

_____

_____

_____

_____

OCTOBER  25

What would you like to tell your father or another close family member?

20_ _ _____

_____
_____
_____
_____

20_ _ _____

_____
_____
_____
_____

20_ _ _____

_____
_____
_____
_____

OCTOBER 26

My grandparent(s) _____.

20__ __ _____

_____

_____

_____

_____

20__ __ _____

_____

_____

_____

_____

20__ __ _____

_____

_____

_____

_____

OCTOBER  27

What do you work hard at?

20_ _ _____

_____

_____

_____

_____

20_ _ _____

_____

_____

_____

_____

20_ _ _____

_____

_____

_____

_____

OCTOBER  28

What would you like to stop from happening?

20___ _____

_____

_____

_____

_____

20___ _____

_____

_____

_____

_____

20___ _____

_____

_____

_____

_____

OCTOBER

29 If one of your parents described you, what would he or she say?

20__ _____

_____

_____

_____

20__ _____

_____

_____

_____

20__ _____

_____

_____

_____

OCTOBER  30

Do you like your room clean or messy?

20___ _____

_____

_____

_____

_____

20___ _____

_____

_____

_____

_____

20___ _____

_____

_____

_____

_____

OCTOBER

31

What Halloween costume did you want to wear? Did you wear it?

20___ _____

_____

_____

_____

_____

20___ _____

_____

_____

_____

_____

20___ _____

_____

_____

_____

_____

NOVEMBER 01

Today I learned _____.

20__ _____

_____

_____

_____

_____

20__ _____

_____

_____

_____

_____

20__ _____

_____

_____

_____

_____

NOVEMBER  02

Have you ever broken a bone or hurt yourself badly? Explain.

20_ _ _____

_____

_____

_____

_____

20_ _ _____

_____

_____

_____

_____

20_ _ _____

_____

_____

_____

_____

NOVEMBER  03

What secret are you
keeping to yourself?

20___ _____

_____

_____

_____

_____

20___ _____

_____

_____

_____

_____

20___ _____

_____

_____

_____

_____

NOVEMBER  04

Which character would you be in a movie or on TV?

20___ _____

_____

_____

_____

_____

20___ _____

_____

_____

_____

_____

20___ _____

_____

_____

_____

_____

NOVEMBER  05

Whom do you like to talk to?

20__ __ _____

_____

_____

_____

20__ __ _____

_____

_____

_____

20__ __ _____

_____

_____

_____

NOVEMBER  06

How is this school year going? Use two words to describe it.

20_ _ _____

_____

_____

_____

_____

20_ _ _____

_____

_____

_____

_____

20_ _ _____

_____

_____

_____

_____

NOVEMBER  07

How do you pass the time on long car rides?

20____ _____

_____

_____

_____

20____ _____

_____

_____

_____

20____ _____

_____

_____

_____

NOVEMBER 08

What are your favorite shoes?

20___ _____

_____

_____

_____

20___ _____

_____

_____

_____

20___ _____

_____

_____

_____

NOVEMBER 09

Today was awesome because _____.

20__ __ _____

_____

_____

_____

20__ __ _____

_____

_____

_____

20__ __ _____

_____

_____

_____

NOVEMBER  10

What is one thing you own that you would never give away?

20___ _____

_____

_____

_____

_____

20___ _____

_____

_____

_____

_____

20___ _____

_____

_____

_____

_____

NOVEMBER  11

Whom would you bring back to life if you could?

20_ _ _ _____

_____

_____

_____

_____

20_ _ _ _____

_____

_____

_____

_____

20_ _ _ _____

_____

_____

_____

_____

NOVEMBER  12

Is something or someone stopping you from doing what you want?

**20__ ** _____

_____

_____

_____

**20__ ** _____

_____

_____

_____

**20__ ** _____

_____

_____

_____

NOVEMBER

Where would you like to go for a family vacation?

20_ _ _____

_____

_____

_____

_____

20_ _ _____

_____

_____

_____

_____

20_ _ _____

_____

_____

_____

_____

NOVEMBER  14

What do you get to do at someone else's house that you wish you could do at yours?

20__ _____

_____

_____

_____

20__ _____

_____

_____

_____

20__ _____

_____

_____

_____

NOVEMBER  15

What is your favorite dessert?

20_ _ _____

_____

_____

_____

_____

20_ _ _____

_____

_____

_____

_____

20_ _ _____

_____

_____

_____

_____

NOVEMBER  16

The two things I'm most afraid of are _____ and _____.

20___ _____

_____

_____

_____

_____

20___ _____

_____

_____

_____

_____

20___ _____

_____

_____

_____

_____

NOVEMBER  17

Describe the room you're in right now.

20__ _____

_____

_____

_____

_____

20__ _____

_____

_____

_____

_____

20__ _____

_____

_____

_____

_____

NOVEMBER 18

I get impatient when _____.

20___ _____

_____

_____

_____

20___ _____

_____

_____

_____

20___ _____

_____

_____

_____

NOVEMBER  19

What advice would
you give to a younger
brother or sister?

20__ _____

_____

_____

_____

_____

20__ _____

_____

_____

_____

_____

20__ _____

_____

_____

_____

_____

NOVEMBER  20

Who are the most important people in your life?

20__ _____

_____

_____

_____

_____

20__ _____

_____

_____

_____

_____

20__ _____

_____

_____

_____

_____

NOVEMBER

21 I feel the happiest when I'm _____.

20____ _____

_____

_____

_____

_____

20____ _____

_____

_____

_____

_____

20____ _____

_____

_____

_____

_____

NOVEMBER  22

What surprised you lately?

20___ _____

_____

_____

_____

_____

20___ _____

_____

_____

_____

_____

20___ _____

_____

_____

_____

_____

NOVEMBER  23

What holiday do you look forward to the most?

20__ _____

_____

_____

_____

_____

20__ _____

_____

_____

_____

_____

20__ _____

_____

_____

_____

_____

NOVEMBER  24

What famous person would you like to talk with?

20__ __ _____

_____

_____

_____

_____

20__ __ _____

_____

_____

_____

_____

20__ __ _____

_____

_____

_____

_____

NOVEMBER 25

My favorite thing to do is _____.

20__ __ _____

_____

_____

_____

_____

20__ __ _____

_____

_____

_____

_____

20__ __ _____

_____

_____

_____

_____

NOVEMBER  26

When did you say something really honest to someone?

20_ _ _____

_____

_____

_____

_____

20_ _ _____

_____

_____

_____

_____

20_ _ _____

_____

_____

_____

_____

NOVEMBER  27

Are you working as hard as you could be? Why or why not?

20___ _____

_____

_____

_____

_____

20___ _____

_____

_____

_____

_____

20___ _____

_____

_____

_____

_____

NOVEMBER  28

When were you goofy?

20_ _ _____

_____

_____

_____

_____

20_ _ _____

_____

_____

_____

_____

20_ _ _____

_____

_____

_____

_____

NOVEMBER 29

Do you usually finish all your homework on time? Explain.

20__ _____

_____

_____

_____

20__ _____

_____

_____

_____

20__ _____

_____

_____

_____

NOVEMBER  **30**

If you could start a company that helped people, how would it help?

20_ _ _____

_____

_____

_____

_____

20_ _ _____

_____

_____

_____

_____

20_ _ _____

_____

_____

_____

_____

DECEMBER  01

Who inspires you?
Why?

20__ __ _____

_____

_____

_____

_____

20__ __ _____

_____

_____

_____

_____

20__ __ _____

_____

_____

_____

_____

DECEMBER

02

Do you like climbing trees and monkey bars? How do you feel about being up high?

20_ _ _____

_____

_____

_____

_____

20_ _ _____

_____

_____

_____

_____

20_ _ _____

_____

_____

_____

_____

DECEMBER  03

How happy are you, on a scale of one to ten?

20__ _____

_____

_____

_____

_____

20__ _____

_____

_____

_____

_____

20__ _____

_____

_____

_____

_____

DECEMBER  04

How do you calm down at night?

20__

_____

20__

_____

20__

_____

DECEMBER  05

Describe an important day in your life.

20__ __ _____

_____

_____

_____

_____

20__ __ _____

_____

_____

_____

_____

20__ __ _____

_____

_____

_____

_____

DECEMBER  06

Who has disappointed
you? How?

20_ _ _____

_____

_____

_____

_____

20_ _ _____

_____

_____

_____

_____

20_ _ _____

_____

_____

_____

_____

DECEMBER  07

If you were invisible today, what would you do?

20_ _ _____

_____

_____

_____

_____

20_ _ _____

_____

_____

_____

_____

20_ _ _____

_____

_____

_____

_____

DECEMBER  08

I want to know _____ better.

20_ _ _____

_____

_____

_____

_____

20_ _ _____

_____

_____

_____

_____

20_ _ _____

_____

_____

_____

_____

DECEMBER  09

Where would you live if you could live anywhere?

20_____

_____

_____

_____

_____

20_____

_____

_____

_____

_____

20_____

_____

_____

_____

_____

DECEMBER  10

Pick a parent. How do you know that parent cares about you?

20__ _____

_____

_____

_____

_____

20__ _____

_____

_____

_____

_____

20__ _____

_____

_____

_____

_____

DECEMBER

What was the most interesting part of school today?

20_ _ _____

_____

_____

_____

_____

20_ _ _____

_____

_____

_____

_____

20_ _ _____

_____

_____

_____

_____

DECEMBER  12

My parents won't
let me _____.

20____ _____

_____

_____

_____

_____

20____ _____

_____

_____

_____

_____

20____ _____

_____

_____

_____

_____

DECEMBER  13

Describe the perfect secret hideout.

20___ _____

_____

_____

_____

_____

20___ _____

_____

_____

_____

_____

20___ _____

_____

_____

_____

_____

DECEMBER  14

If anyone knew I _____,
they'd think I was nuts.

20__ _____

_____

_____

_____

20__ _____

_____

_____

_____

20__ _____

_____

_____

_____

DECEMBER  15

What do you daydream about?

20__ _____

_____

_____

_____

_____

20__ _____

_____

_____

_____

_____

20__ _____

_____

_____

_____

_____

DECEMBER  16

_____ is boring to me because _____.

20___ _____

_____

_____

_____

20___ _____

_____

_____

_____

20___ _____

_____

_____

_____

DECEMBER  17

What do you like to talk about with your friends?

20__ __ _____

_____

_____

_____

_____

20__ __ _____

_____

_____

_____

_____

20__ __ _____

_____

_____

_____

_____

DECEMBER  18

Describe the weather outside.

20___ _____

_____

_____

_____

_____

20___ _____

_____

_____

_____

_____

20___ _____

_____

_____

_____

_____

DECEMBER  19

What did you do to get
some exercise today?

20__ __ _____

_____

_____

_____

_____

20__ __ _____

_____

_____

_____

_____

20__ __ _____

_____

_____

_____

_____

DECEMBER  20

Have you ever been on an airplane or a train? Where did you go and what was it like?

20_ _ _____

_____

_____

_____

_____

20_ _ _____

_____

_____

_____

_____

20_ _ _____

_____

_____

_____

_____

DECEMBER  21

What is your favorite day of the week? Why?

20___ _____

_____

_____

_____

_____

20___ _____

_____

_____

_____

_____

20___ _____

_____

_____

_____

_____

DECEMBER  22

What is the worst thing that could happen to you?

20___ _____

_____

_____

_____

_____

20___ _____

_____

_____

_____

_____

20___ _____

_____

_____

_____

_____

DECEMBER  23

_____ is a habit that I would like to break.

**20__ ** _____

_____

_____

_____

_____

**20__ ** _____

_____

_____

_____

_____

**20__ ** _____

_____

_____

_____

_____

DECEMBER  24

Someone who knew me well would describe me using these two words: _____ and _____.

20_ _ _____

_____

_____

_____

_____

20_ _ _____

_____

_____

_____

_____

20_ _ _____

_____

_____

_____

_____

DECEMBER  25

What are you looking forward to?

20__ __ _____

_____

_____

_____

_____

20__ __ _____

_____

_____

_____

_____

20__ __ _____

_____

_____

_____

_____

DECEMBER  26

What would you like to invent?

20__ _____

_____

_____

_____

_____

20__ _____

_____

_____

_____

_____

20__ _____

_____

_____

_____

_____

DECEMBER 27

If I were older, I would
_____.

20___ _____

_____

_____

_____

_____

20___ _____

_____

_____

_____

_____

20___ _____

_____

_____

_____

_____

DECEMBER  28

What have you always had trouble with?

20__ _____

_____

_____

_____

_____

20__ _____

_____

_____

_____

_____

20__ _____

_____

_____

_____

_____

DECEMBER  29

Has anyone said something really nice to you lately? What was it?

20_ _ _____

_____

_____

_____

_____

20_ _ _____

_____

_____

_____

_____

20_ _ _____

_____

_____

_____

_____

DECEMBER  30

Describe your favorite place at home.

20_ _ _____

_____

_____

_____

_____

20_ _ _____

_____

_____

_____

_____

20_ _ _____

_____

_____

_____

_____

DECEMBER  Draw a picture of yourself.

20___

20___

20___

POTTER STYLE

www.crownpublishing.com
www.potterstyle.com

ISBN 978-0-307-95296-7
Printed in China

10
First Edition